# AN ACCOUNT OF THE ROMANSH LANGUAGE

# LECTOR HOUSE PUBLIC DOMAIN WORKS

# AN ACCOUNT OF THE ROMANSH LANGUAGE.

## JOSEPH PLANTA

ISBN: 978-93-5342-106-9

First Published:     -

© LECTOR HOUSE LLP

LECTOR HOUSE LLP
E-MAIL: lectorpublishing@gmail.com

# AN ACCOUNT OF THE
# ROMANSH LANGUAGE.

BY

JOSEPH PLANTA, ESQ. F. R. S.

# AN ACCOUNT OF THE ROMANSH LANGUAGE.

*In a Letter to Sir John Pringle, Bart. P. R. S.*
[Handwriting: Phil. Trans. vol LXVI. A.D. 1776]

British Museum,
June 30, 1775.

SIR,

The Bible lately presented to the Royal Society by Count de Salis, being a version into a language as little attended to in this country, as it may appear curious to those who take pleasure in philological inquiries; I embrace this opportunity to communicate to you, and, with your approbation, to the Society, all that I have been able to collect concerning its history and present state.

This language is called *Romansh*, and is now spoken in the most mountainous parts of the country of the Grisons, near the sources of the Rhine and the Inn. It consists of two main dialects; which, though partaking both of the above general name, differ however so widely as to constitute in a manner two distinct languages. Books are printed in both of them; and each, though it be universally understood in its respective district, is yet sub-divided into almost as many secondary dialects as there are villages in which it is spoken; which differ, however, but little except in the pronunciation. One of the main dialects, which is spoken in the Engadine, a valley extending from the source of the Inn to the frontiers of the Tyrolese, is by the inhabitants called *Ladin*. It admits of some variation, even in the books, according as they are printed either in the upper or the lower part of this province. The abovementioned Bible is in the dialect of the lower Engadine; which, however, is perfectly understood in the upper part of that province, where they use no other version. The other dialect, which is the language of the Grey, or Upper. League, is distinguished from the former by the name of *Cialover*:[1] and I must here observe, that in the very centre, and most inaccessible parts of this latter district, there are some villages situated in the narrow valleys, called Rheinwald, Cepina,[2] &c. in which a third language is spoken, more similar to the German than to either of the above idioms, although they be neither contiguous, nor have any great intercourse with the parts where the German is used.

It being impossible to form any idea of the origin and progress of a language,

---

[1] This is rather a trivial name; but the dialect has no other distinctive appellation.
[2] Tschudi, Rhæt. Descrip. p. 43, MERIN Topogr. Helvet. p. 64.

without attending to the revolutions that may have contributed to its formation and subsequent variations; and this being particularly the case in the present instance, wherein no series of documents is extant to guide us in our researches; I shall briefly recapitulate the principal events which may have affected the language of the Grisons, as I find them related by authors of approved veracity.[3]

Ambigatus, the first king of the Celtic Gaul upon record, who[4] about 400[5] years before Christ, governed all the country situated between the Alps and the Pyrenaean mountains, sent out two formidable armies under the command of one of his nephews; one of whom, named Segovisius, forced his way into the heart of Germany: and the other, Bellovisius, having passed the Alps, penetrated into Italy as far as the settlements of the Tuscans, which at that time extended over the greatest part of the country now called Lombardy. These, and several other swarms of invaders whom the successes of the former soon after attracted, having totally subdued that country, built Milan, Verona, Brescia, and several other considerable towns, and governed with such tyrannic sway, especially over the nobility, whose riches they coveted and sought by every means to extort from them, that most of the principal families, joining under the conduct of Rhætus[6], one of the most distinguished personages among them, retired with the best part of their effects and attendants among the steepest mountains of the Alps, near the sources of the Rhine, into the district which is now called the Grey League.

The motive of their flight, their civil deportment, and perhaps more so, the wealth they brought with them, procured them a favourable reception from the original inhabitants of that inhospitable region, who are mentioned by authors[7] as being a Celtic nation, fabulously conjectured from their name [Greek: leipontio][8] to have been left there by Hercules in his expedition into Spain.

The new adventurers had no sooner climbed over the highest precipices, but thinking themselves secure from the pursuits of their rapacious enemies, they fixed in a valley which, from its great fertility in comparison of the country they had just passed, they called Domestica[9]. They intermixed with the old inhabitants, and built some towns and many castles, whose present names manifestly bespeak their origin.[10] They soon after spread all over the country, which took the

---

[3] Sprecher, Simler, Tschudi, Scheuchzer. Campell's Chronicle is looked upon as the most authentic and circumstantial; but there being only a few manuscript copies of it extant in the hands of private persons in the Grisons, I have not been able to avail myself of his researches. Guller and Stumpfius might also have furnished some material information; but neither of them have I had an opportunity of inspecting.

[4] Liv. lib. v. c. 34.

[5] Other authors place the reign of this king 180 years earlier.

[6] Plin. lib. iii. c. 5. Justin. lib. xx. c. 5.

[7] Cluver, Ital. Antiq. lib. i. c. 14.

[8] A spurious derivation from the verb [Greek: leipo].

[9] Probably by them pronounced Tomiliasca, *the name* it now bears.

[10] Tusis (Tu*scia*) and in Italian Tosana, *the principal* place; Rhealta (*Rhetia* alta); Rheambs (*Rhetia* ampla); Rhazunz (*Rhetia* ima); and above twelve other castles, the remains of which are now to be seen in the valley Tomiliasca.

name of Rhaetia from that of their leader; and introduced a form of government similar to their own, of which there are evident traces at this day, especially in the administration of justice; in which a *Laertes* or president, now called landamman or ministral, together with twelve *Lucumones*[11] or jurors, determine all causes, both civil and criminal:[12] and Livy,[13] although he erroneously pretends that they retained none of their ancient customs, yet allows that they continued the use of their language, though somewhat adulterated by a mixture with that of the Aborigines.

I must here interrupt the thread of this narration by observing, that the only way to account for the present use of a different language in the centre and most craggy parts of the Grey League, is by allowing that the Tuscans, who, from the delicacy of their constitutions and habits, were little able, and less inclined, to encounter the hardships of so severe a climate and so barren a soil, never attempted to mix with the original and more sturdy inhabitants of that unfavoured spot; but left them and their language, which could only be a Celtic idiom, in the primitive state in which they found them.[14]

But to proceed;—several Roman families, dreading the fury of the Carthaginians under Hannibal, and perhaps, since during the rage of the civil wars, and the subsequent oppressive reigns, interior commotions and foreign invasions, forsook the Latium and Campania, and resorted for a peaceful enjoyment of their liberty, some into the islands where Venice now stands, and many into the mountains of the Grisons, where they chiefly fixed their residence in the Engadine,[15] as appears not only from the testimonies of authors,[16] but also from the names of several places and families which are evidently of Roman derivation.[17]

The inhabitants these emigrants found in that place of refuge could not but be a mixture of the Tuscans and original Lepontii; and the two languages which met upon this occasion must, at the very first, have had some affinity; as the Tuscan, which derived immediately from the Greek, is known to have had a great share in the formation of the Roman. But as it is generally observed, that the more polished people introduce their native tongue wherever they go to reside in any considerable numbers, the arrival of these successive colonies must gradually have produced a considerable change in the language of the country in which they settled;[18] and this change gave rise to the dialect since called Ladin, probably from the name of the mother country of its principal authors.[19]

[11] In some communities there are fourteen jurors besides the Landamman.

[12] Serv. in Æneid. lib. viii. 65. lib. x. 202. Sprech. Pall. Rhæt p. 9. Siml. Rep. Helv. p. 281. ed. 1735.

[13] Liv. lib. v. c. 33.

[14] Sprech. p. 214. Mer. l. c.

[15] *En Code Ino*, perhaps the vulgar Roman phrase expressing *In Capite Oeni*. There are other etymologies, but all equally uncertain.

[16] Sprech. p. 10.

[17] *Lavin* (Lavinium), *Sus* (Susa), *Zernetz* (Cerneto), *Ardetz* (Ardea), &c.

[18] Sprech. p. 10.

[19] A parallel instance of the formation of a language by Roman colonies is the idiom

Although the name of *Romansh*, which the whole language bears, seems to be a badge of Roman servitude, yet the conquest of that nation, if ever effected, could not have produced a great alteration in a language which must already have been so similar to their own; and its general name may as well be attributed to the pacific as to the hostile Romans. But when we consider that a coalition of the two main dialects, which differ so far as not to be reciprocally understood, must have been the inevitable consequence of a total reduction; and that such a coalition is known never to have taken place, we may lay the greater stress upon the many passages of ancient authors,[20] in which it is implied that the boasted victories of the Romans over the Rhaeti, for which public honours had been decreed to L. Munatus, M. Anthony, Drusus, and Augustus, amounted to no more than frequent repulses of those hardy people into their mountains; out of which their want of sufficient room and sustenance, (which in our days drives considerable numbers into the services of foreign powers) compelled them at times to make desperate excursions in quest of necessaries. And we may also from these collected authorities be induced to give the greater credit to the commentator of Lucan,[21] and to the modern historians,[22] who positively assert, that the people living near the sources of the Rhine and the Inn were never totally subdued by the Roman arms; but only repelled in their attempts to harass their neighbours.

This whole country, however, from its central situation, could not but be annumerated to one of the provinces of the empire; and accordingly we find that Rhaetia itself (which by the accounts of ancient geographers[23] appears to have extended its limits beyond the lake of Constance, Augsburg, and Trent, towards Germany, and to Como and Verona towards Italy) was formed into a Roman province, governed by a pro-consul or procurator, who resided at Augsburg; and that when in the year 119, the Emperor Adrian divided it into Rhaetia *prima* and *secunda*, the governor of the former, in which the country I am now speaking of must have been comprized, took up his residence in two castles situated where Coire now stands, whilst the other continued his seat at Augsburg. But notwithstanding these appearances, no trace or monument of Roman servitude is to be met with in

---

of Moldavia; which, according to Prince Cantemir's account of that country, has still many traces of its Latin origin, and which, though engrafted upon the Dacian, and since upon the Sclavonian dialects of the Celtic, may still be considered as a sister language to that I am, here treating of.

[20] Videre Rhaeti bella *sub* Alpibus

    Drusum gerentem et Vindelici. HOR. lib. 4. Od. iv.

      — — — — —- immanesque Rhaetos

    Auspiciis *repulit* secundis. Ibid. Od. xiv.

    Fundat ab extremo flavos aquilone Suevos

    Albis, et *indomitum Rheni Caput.* Luc. lib. ii. 52.

      — — — — — —- Rhenumque minacem *Cornibus infractis.*

    CLAUD. Laud. Stilich. lib. i. 220.

[21] Horten. in Lucan, p. 163. edit. 1578. fol.

[22] Sprech. p. 18. &c.

[23] Strabo, lib. IV, sub. fin. Cluver. Ital. vet. lib. I. c. 16.

this district, except the ambiguous name of one mountain,[24] situated on the skirts of these highlands, and generally thought to have been the *non plus ultra* of the Roman arms on the Italian side.

From the difficulty those persevering veterans experienced in keeping this stubborn people in awe, I mean to infer that such strenuous asserters of their independence, whom the flattering pens of Ovid and Horace represent as formidable even to Augustus, and preferring death to the loss of their liberties,[25] favoured by the natural strength and indigence of their country, were not very likely to be so far subdued by any foreign power inferior to the Roman, as to suffer any considerable revolution in their customs and language: for as to the irruptions of the Goths, Vandals, and Lombards, in the fifth and sixth centuries, besides a profound silence in history concerning any successful attempt of those barbarians upon this spot, it is scarce credible, that any of them should have either wished or endeavoured to settle in a country, perhaps far less hospitable than that which they had just forsaken, especially after they had opened to themselves a way into the fertile plains of Lombardy.

Some stress must be laid upon this inference, as the history of what befel this country after the decline of the Roman empire is so intimately blended with that of Suabia, the Tyrolese, and the lower parts of the Grisons, which are known to have fallen to the share of the rising power of the Franks, that nothing positive can be drawn from authors as to the interior state of this small tract. The victory gained in the year 496 near Cologn, by Clovis I. king of the Franks, over the Alemanni, who had wrested from the Romans all the dominions on the northern side of the Alps; and the defeat of both Romans and Goths in Italy, in the year 549, by the treacherous arms of Theodebert king of Austrasia, whose dominions soon after devolved to the crown of France, necessarily gave the aspiring Merovingian race a great ascendency over all the countries surrounding the Grisons; and accordingly we find, that this district also was soon after, without any military effort, considered as part of the dominions of the reviving western empire. But it does not appear that those monarchs ever made any other use of their supremacy in these parts than, agreeably to the feudal system which they introduced, to constitute dukes, earls, presidents, and bailiffs, over Rhaetia; to grant out tenures upon the usual feudal terms; and consequently to levy forces in most of their military expeditions.

It must, however, be observed, that these feudal substitutes were seldom, if ever, strangers: those who are upon record to the latter end of the eighth century, having all been chosen from among the nobility of the country.[26] And that no foreign garrisons were ever maintained for any continuance of time in these parts, appears from a circumstance related by their annalists;[27] who say, that an inroad of the Huns in 670, when external forces would probably have been very acceptable to the natives, was repulsed merely by a concourse of the inhabitants.

[24] Julius Mo*ns*, *Scheuchzer* Iter. Alp. p. 114.

[25] Rhaetica nunc praebent Thraciaque arma metum. OVID. Trist. lib. ii. 226. Devota morti pectora liberae. HOR. 4. lib. Od. xiv.

[26] Sprech. p. 52-55.

[27] Sprech. p. 58.

History continues to furnish us with proofs of the little connexion this people had with other nations in their domestic affairs, notwithstanding their dependance upon a foreign power. In the year 780, the Bishop of Coire, who by the constitution of that see can only be a native,[28] obtained from Charlemain, besides many considerable honours and privileges in the empire, a grant of the supreme authority in this country, by the investiture of the office of hereditary president or bailiff over all Rhaetia. His successors not only enjoyed this prerogative to the extinction of the Carlovingian race of emperors in 911; but received accumulated favours from other succeeding monarchs, as the bigoted devotion of those times or motives of interest prompted them. And so far did their munificence gradually extend, that the sole property of one of the three leagues[29] was at one time vested in the hands of the bishop.

This prelate and the nobles, the greatest part of whom became his retainers, availed themselves, like all the German princes, of the confusion, divisions, and interreigns which frequently distracted the empire in the succeeding centuries, in order to establish a firm and unlimited authority of their own. Henceforth the annals of this country furnish us with little more than catalogues of the bishops and dukes, who were still, at times, nominated by the emperors; and of the domains granted out by them to different indigenate families; with accounts of the atrocious cruelties exercised by these lords over their vassals; and with anecdotes of the prowess of the natives in several expeditions into Italy and Palestine, in which they still voluntarily accompanied the emperors.

The repeated acts of tyranny exercised by those arbitrary despots, who had now shaken off all manner of restraint, at length exasperated the people into a general revolt, and brought on the confederacy; in which the bishop and most of the nobles were glad to join, in order to screen themselves from the fury of the insurgents.

The first step towards this happy revolution was made by some *venerable old men dressed in the coarse grey cloth* of the country, who in the year 1424 met privately in a wood near a place called Truns, in the Upper League; where, *impressed with a sense of their former liberties,*[30] they determined to remonstrate against, and oppose, the violent proceedings of their oppressors. The abbot Dissentis was the first who countenanced their measures; their joint influence gradually prevailed over several of the most moderate among the nobles; and hence arose the league which, from the colour of its first promoters, was ever called the Grey League; which, from its being the first in the bold attempt to shake off the yoke of wanton tyranny, has ever since retained the pre-eminence in rank before the two other leagues; and which has even given its name to the whole country, whose inhabitants, from the circumstances of their deliverance, pride themselves in the appellation of *Grisones*,

---

[28] This privilege has at times been waved; but never without some plausible pretence, and a formal rescript acknowledging the exclusive right.

[29] The League Cadéa, or *of the* House of God, *so called* from the cathedral of the bishopric of Coire, which is situated in its capital.

[30] Canitie griseoque amictu venerandi.—Memores adhuc antiquae libertatis. Sprech. p. 189.

or the *grey-ones*.[31] From this period nothing has ever affected their freedom and absolute independence, which they now enjoy in the most unlimited sense, in spite of the repeated efforts of the house of Austria to recover some degree of ascendency over them.

From this concise view of the history of the Grisons, in which I have carefully guarded against favouring any particular hypothesis, it appears, that as no foreign nation ever gained any permanent footing in the most mountainous parts of this country since the establishment of the Tuscans and Romans, the language now spoken could never have suffered any considerable alterations from extraneous mixtures of modern languages. And to those who may object, that languages like all other human institutions will, though left to themselves, be inevitably affected by the common revolutions of time, I shall observe, that a language, in which no books are written, but which is only spoken by a people chiefly devoted to arms and agriculture, and consequently not cultivated by the criticisms of men of taste and learning, is by no means exposed to the vicissitudes of those that are polished by refined nations;[32] and that, however paradoxical it may appear, it is nevertheless true, that the degeneracy of a language is more frequently to be attributed to an extravagant refinement than to the neglect of an illiterate people, unless indeed external causes interfere. May we not hence conclude, that as the Romansh has never been used in any regular composition in writing till the sixteenth century, nor affected by any foreign invasion or intimate connexion, it is not likely to have received any material change before the period of its being written? And we have the authority of the books since printed to prove, that it is at present the identical language that was spoken two hundred years ago. These arguments will receive additional weight from the proofs I shall hereafter give of the great affinity there is between the language as it is now spoken, and the Romance that was used in France nine centuries ago.

When we further consider the facts I have above briefly related, the wonder will cease, that in a cluster of mountains, situated in the centre of Europe, a distinct language (not a dialect or jargon of those spoken by the contiguous nations, as has been generally imagined) should have maintained itself through a series of ages, in spite of the many revolutions which frequently changed the whole face of the adjacent countries. And indeed, so obstinately tenacious are these people of their independency, laws, customs, and consequently of their very language, that, as has been already observed, their form of government, especially in judicial matters, still bears evident marks of the ancient Tuscan constitution; and that, although they be frequently exposed to inconveniences from their stubbornness in this respect, they have not yet been prevailed upon to adopt the Gregorian reformation of the calendar.

As to the nature of this language, it may now be advanced, with some degree

------

[31] The following barbarous distich is sometimes inscribed on the arms of the three leagues. Foedera sunt cana, cana fides, cana libertas: Haec tria sub uno continentur corpore Rhaeto.

[32] See Dr. Percy's preface to his translation of Mallet's Northern Antiquities, p. xxii. where this question is more amply discussed.

of confidence, that the *Cialover* owes it origin to a mixture of the Tuscan and of the dialect of the Celtic spoken by the Lepontii; and that the introduction of the vulgar Roman affected it in some degree, but particularly gave rise to the *Ladin*; the vocabulary of which, as any one may be convinced by inspecting a few lines of the bible, has a great affinity with that of the Latin tongue. But these assertions rest merely upon historical evidence; for as to the *Cialover*, all that it may have retained of the Tuscan or Roman, is so much disfigured by an uncouth pronunciation and a vague orthography, that all etymological inquiries are thereby rendered intricate and unsatisfactory. And as to the *Ladin*, although its derivation be more manifest, yet we are equally at a loss from what period or branch of the Latin tongue to trace its real origin; for I have found, after many tedious experiments, that even the vocabulary, in which the resemblance is most evident, differs equally from the classical purity of Tully, Caesar, and Sallust, as it does from the primitive Latin of the twelve tables, of Ennius, and the *columna rostralis* of Duillius, which has generally been thought the parent of the Gallic Romance; as also from the trivial language of Varro, Vegetius, and Columella. May we not from this circumstance infer, that, as is the case in all vernacular tongues, the vulgar dialect of the Romans, the *sermo usualis, rusticus, pedestris*,[33] of which there are no monuments extant, differed very widely both in pronunciation and construction from that which has at any time been used either in writing or in the senate?

The grammatical variations, the syntax, and the genius of the language, must in this, as well as in several other modern European tongues, have been derived from the Celtic; it being well known, that the frequent use of articles, the distinction of cases by prepositions, the application of two auxiliaries in the conjugations, do by no means agree with the Latin turn of expression; although a late French academician[34] who has taken great pains to prove that the Gallic Romance was solely derived from the Roman, quotes several instances in which even the most classical writers have in this respect offended the purity of that refined language. It cannot here be denied, that as new ideas always require new signs to express them, some foreign words, and perhaps phrases, must necessarily, from time to time, have insinuated themselves into the Romansh, by the military and some commercial intercourse of the Grisons with other nations; and this accounts for several modern German words which are now incorporated into the language of the Engadine.[35]

The little connexion there is in mountainous countries between the inhabitants of the different valleys, and the absolute independence of each jurisdiction in this district, which still lessens the frequency of their intercourse, also accounts, in a great measure, for the variety of secondary dialects subsisting in almost every different community or even village.

The oldest specimens of writing in this language are some dramatical performances in verse upon scriptural subjects, which are extant only in manuscript. The

[33] Conf. Mem. des Inscrip. tom. xxiv. p. 608.

[34] Bonamy, v. Mem. des Inscrip. l. c.

[35] Tapferdà, *Trapfer*keit, Bravery; Nardà, Nar*heit,* Folly; Klinot, K*leinod,* a Jewel; Graf, Graf, *a* Count; Baur, Baur, *a* Peasant, &c.

Histories of Susanna, of the Prodigal Son, of Judith and Holofernes, and of Esther, are among the first; and are said to have been composed about the year 1560. The books that have since been printed are chiefly upon religious subjects; and among those that are not so, the only I have ever heard of are a small code of the laws of the country in the Cialover dialect, and an epitome of Sprecher's Chronicle, by Da Porta, in the Ladin.

*      *      *      *      *

The language spoken in Gaul from the fifth to the twelfth centuries being evidently a mixture of the same Roman and Celtic ingredients, and partaking of the same name with those of the Grisons; it will, I hope, not be thought foreign to the subject of this letter, if I enter into a few particulars concerning it, as it seems to have been an essential part, or rather the trunk, of the language, the history of which I am endeavouring to elucidate.

One of the many instances how little the laboured researches of philologists into the origin of languages are to be depended upon, is the variety of opinions entertained by French authors concerning the formation of the Gallic Romance. A learned Benedictine[36] first starts the conjecture, and then maintains it against the attacks of an anonymous writer, that the vulgar Latin became the universal language of Gaul immediately after Caesar's conquest, and that its corruption, with very little mixture of the original language of the country, gradually produced the Romance towards the eighth century. Bonamy,[37] on the other hand, is of opinion, that soon after that conquest, a corruption of vulgar Latin by the Celtic formed the Romance, which he takes to be the language always meant by authors when they speak of the *Lingua Romana* used in Gaul. The author of the Celtic Dictionary[38] tells us, that the Romance is derived from the *Latin*, the *Celtic*, which he more frequently calls Gallic, and the *Teutonic*; in admitting of which latter he deviates from most other authors,[39] who deny that the Teutonic had any share in the composition of the Romance, since the Franks found it already established when they entered Gaul, and were long before they could prevail upon their new subjects to adopt any part of their own mother tongue, which however appears to have been afterwards instrumental in the formation of the modern French. Duclos,[40] guided, I imagine, by du Cange,[41] whose opinion appears to be the most sober and best authenticated, maintains that the vulgar Latin was undoubtedly the foundation of the Romance; but that much of the Celtic gradually insinuated itself in spite of the policy of the Romans, who never failed to use all their endeavours in order to establish their language wherever they spread their arms.

Among this variety of conjectures and acute controversies, I find it however agreed on all hands, that the vocabulary of the Roman, and the idiom of the Celtic,

[36] Rivet, Hist. Litt. de la France, tom. vii. p. 1. et seq.
[37] Mem. des Inscrip. tom. xxiv. p. 594.
[38] Bullet, Mem. de la Langue Celtique, tom. i. p. 23.
[39] Mem. des Inscrip. tom. xxiv. p. 603.
[40] Mem. des. Inscrip. tom. xv. p. 575. et seq.
[41] Praef. Gloss. n. xiii.

have chiefly contributed to the formation of the Gallic, Romance, which is sufficient to prove that it partakes of a common origin with that of the Grisons.

There are incontestable proofs that this language was once universal all over France; and that this, and not immediately the Latin, has been the parent of the Provençal, and afterwards of the modern French, the Italian, and the Spanish. The oath taken by Lewis the Germanic, in the year 842, in confirmation of an alliance between him and Charles the Bald his brother, is a decisive proof of the general use of the Romance by the whole French nation at that time, and of their little knowledge of the Teutonic, which being the native tongue of Lewis, would certainly have been used by him, in this oath, had it been understood by the French to whom he addressed himself. But Nithardus,[42] a contemporary writer and near relation to the contracting parties, informs us, that Lewis took the oath in the Romance language, in order that it might be understood by the French nobility who were the subjects of Charles; and that they, in their turn, entered into reciprocal engagements in *their own language*, which the same author again declares to have been the Romance, and not the Teutonic; although one would imagine that, had they at all understood this latter tongue, they could not but have used it upon this occasion, in return for the condescension of Lewis.

As a comparison between this language and the Romansh of the Grisons cannot be considered as a mere object of curiosity, but may also serve to corroborate the proofs I have above alleged of the antiquity of the latter, I have annexed in the appendix,[43] a translation of this oath into the language of Engadine, which approaches nearest to it; although I must observe, that there are in the other dialect some words which have a still greater affinity with the language of the oath, as appears by another translation I have procured, in which both dialects are indifferently used. To prevent any doubts concerning the veracity of these translations, I must here declare, that I am indebted for them, and for several anecdotes concerning that language, to a man of letters, who is a native and has long been an inhabitant of the Grisons, and is lately come to reside in London. I have added to this comparative view of those two languages, the Latin words from which both seem to have been derived; and, as a proof of the existence of the Gallic Romance in France down to the twelfth century, I have also subjoined the words used in that kingdom at that period, as they are given us by the author of the article *(Langue) Romane*, in the French Encyclopedie.

To the comparison of the two Romances, and the similarity of their origin, I may now with confidence add the authority of Fontanini[44] to prove, that they are one and the same language. This author, speaking of the ancient Gallic Romance, asserts that it is now spoken in the country of the Grisons; though, not attending to the variety of dialects, some of which have certainly nothing of the Italian, he supposes it to have been altogether adulterated by a mixture of that modern tongue.

Whilst the Grisons neglected to improve their language, and rejected, or in-

---

[42] Du Chesne, Hist. Franc. tom. ii. p. 374.
[43] No. I.
[44] Eloq. Ital. p. 44.

deed were out of the reach of every refinement it might have derived from polished strangers, the taste and fertile genius of the Troubadours, fostered by the countenance and elegance of the brilliant courts and splendid nobility of Provence, did not long leave theirs in the rough state in which we find it in the ninth century. But the change having been gradual and almost imperceptible, the French historians have fixed no epocha for the transition of the Romance into the Provençal. That the former language had not received any considerable alteration in the twelfth Century may be gathered from the comparison in the appendix: and, that it still bore the same name, appears from the titles of several books which are said to have been written in, or translated into, the Romance. But though mention is made of that name even after this aera, yet upon examining impartially what is given us for that language in this period, it will be found so different from the Romance of the ninth century, that to trace it any further would be both a vain and an extravagant pursuit.

Admitting, however, the universal use of the Romance all over France down to the twelfth century, which no French author has yet doubted or denied; and allowing that what the writers of those times say of the Gallic is to be understood of the Romance, as appears from chronological proofs, and the expressions of several authors prior to the fifth century;[45] who, by distinguishing the *Gallic* both from the *Latin* and the *Celtic*, plainly indicate that they thereby mean the Romance, those being the only three languages which, before the invasion of the Franks, could possibly have been spoken, or even understood in Gaul: admitting these premises, I say, it necessarily follows, that the language introduced into England under Alfred, and afterwards more universally established by Edward the Confessor, and William the Conqueror, must have been an emanation of the Romance, very near akin to that of the abovementioned oath, and consequently to that which is now spoken in the Alps.

The intercourse between Britain and Gaul is known to have been of a very early date; for even in the first century we find, that the British lawyers derived the greatest part of their knowledge from those of the continent;[46] while on the other hand, the Gallic Druids are known to have resorted to Britain for instruction in their mysterious rites. The Britons, therefore, could not be totally ignorant of the Gallic language. And hence it will appear, that Grimbald, John, and the other doctors introduced by Alfred,[47] could find no great difficulty in propagating their native tongue in this island; which tongue, at that interval of time, could only be the true Romance, since they were contemporaries with Lewis the Germanic.

That the Romance was almost universally understood in this kingdom under Edward the Confessor, it being not only used at court, but frequently at the bar, and even sometimes in the pulpit, is a fact too well known and attested[48] to need

[45] Fidei commissa quocunque Sermone relinqui possunt, non solum *Latino* vel Graeco, sed etiam Punico vel *Gallicano*. Digest. l. xxii. tit. 1. sec. 11. Tu autem vel *Celtice*, vel si mavis *Gallice*, loquere. Sulp. Sev. Dial, i, sec. 6. sub sin.

[46] Gallia Causidicos docuit facunda Britannos. Juv. Sat. xv. 111.

[47] William of Malmsb. l. ii. c. 4.

[48] Ingulph. passim. Du Chesne, tom. iii.

my further authenticating it with superfluous arguments and testimonies.

Duclos, in his History of the Gallic' Romance,[49] gives the abovementioned oath of Lewis as the first monument of that language. The second he mentions is the code of laws of William the Conqueror,[50] whom the least proficient in the English history knows to have rendered his language almost universal in this kingdom. How little progress it had yet made towards the modern French; and how great an affinity it still bore with the present Romansh of the Grisons, will appear from the annexed translation of the first paragraph of these laws into the latter tongue.[51]

If we may credit Du Cange,[52] who grounds his assertion upon various instruments of the kings of Scotland during the twelfth century, the Romance had also penetrated into that kingdom before that period.

The same corruption, or coalescence, which gave rise to the Gallic Romance, and to that of the Grisons, must also have produced in Italy a language, if not perfectly similar, at least greatly approaching to those two idioms. Nor did it want its northern nations to contribute what the two other branches derived from that source.[53] But be the origin what it will, certain it is, that a jargon very different from either the Latin or the Italian was spoken in Italy from the time of the irruptions of the barbarians to the successful labours of Dante and Petrarca; that this jargon was usually called the *vulgar idiom*; but that Speroni,[54] the father of an Italian literature, and others, frequently call it the *common Italian Romance*. And if Fontanini's[55] authorities be sufficient, it appears that even the Gallic Romance, by the residence of the papal court at Avignon, and from other causes, made its way into Italy before it was polished into the Provençal.

As to Naples and Sicily, the expulsion of the Saracens by the Normans, under Robert Guiscard in 1059, must have produced in that country nearly the same effect, a similar event soon after brought about in England. And in fact we have the authority of William of Apulia[56] to prove, that the conquerors used all their efforts to propagate their language and manners among the natives, that they might ever after be considered only as one people. And Hugo Falcland[57] relates, that in the year 1150, Count Henry refused to take upon him the management of public affairs, under pretence of not knowing the language of the French; which, he adds, was absolutely necessary at court.

That the language of the Romans penetrated very early into Spain, appears

---

[49] Mem. des Inscrip. tom. xvii. p. 179.

[50] Wilkins, Leges Anglo-Sax.

[51] Append. No, II.

[52] Praef. Gloss, n. xxi.

[53] Fontanini, p. 4.

[54] Speron. Dial, passim.—Conf. Menage, Orig. della Ling Ital. voce Romanza.

[55] Font. p. 17.

[56] Murat. Scrip. Ital. tom. v. p. 255.

[57] Ibid. tom. vii. p. 322.

most evidently from a passage in Strabo,[58] who asserts that the Turditani inhabiting the banks of the Boetis, now the Guadalquivir, forgot their original tongue, and adopted that of the conquerors. That the Romance was used there in the fourteenth century appears from a correspondence between St. Vincent of Ferrieres and Don Martin, son of Peter the IVth of Arragon;[59] and that this language must once have been common in that kingdom appears manifestly from the present name of the Spanish, which is still usually called Romance.[60] These circumstances considered, I am not so much inclined to discredit a fact related by Mabillon,[61] who says, that in the eighth century a paralytic Spaniard, on paying his devotions at the tomb of a saint in the church of Fulda, conversed with a monk of that abbey, who, *because he was an Italian*, understood the language of the Spaniard. Neither does an oral tradition I heard some times ago appear so absurd to me, as it did when it was first related to me, which says, that two Catalonians travelling over the Alps, were not a little surprized when they came into the Grison country, to find that their native tongue was understood by the inhabitants, and that they could comprehend most of the language of that district.

This universality of the Romance in the French dominions during the eleventh century, also accounts for its introduction in Palestine and many other parts of the Levant by Godfrey de Bouillon, and the multitude of adventurers who engaged under him in the Crusade. The assizes of Jerusalem, and those of Cyprus, are standing monuments of the footing that language had obtained in those parts; and if we may trust a Spanish historian of some reputation[62] who resided in Greece in the thirteenth century, the Athenians and the inhabitants of Morea spoke at that time the same language that was used in France. And there is great reason to imagine, that the affinity the *Lingua Franca* bears to the French and Italian is intirely to be derived from the Romance, which was once commonly used in the ports of the Levant. The heroic atchievements and gallantry of the knights of the cross also gave rise to the swarm of fabulous narratives; which, though not an invention of those days, were yet, from the name of the language in which they were written, ever after distinguished by the appellation of *Romances*.[63]

I shall now conclude this letter by observing, that far from presuming that the Romance has been preserved so near its primitive state only in the country of the Grisons, there is great reason to suppose that it still exists in several other remote and unfrequented parts. When Fontanini informs us[64] that the ancient Romance is now spoken in the country of the Grisons, he adds, that it is also the common dialect of the Friulese, and of some districts in Savoy bordering upon Dauphiné. And Rivet[65] seriously undertakes to prove, that the Patois of several parts of the

[58] Lib. iii.
[59] Mabil. an. l. 64, n. 124.
[60] Orozco, Tes. Castill. voce Romance—Conf. Crescimb. Volg. Poes. l. v. c. 1.
[61] Act. Ben. Saec. 3. p. 2. p. 258.
[62] Raym. Montanero Chronica de Juan I.
[63] Huet, Orig. des Rom. p. 126. ed. 1678.
[64] P. 43, 44.
[65] Hist. Litt. de la Fr. tom. vii. p. 22.

Limousin, Quercy, and Auvergne (which in fact agrees singularly with the *Romansh* of the Grisons) is the very Romance of eight centuries ago. Neither do I doubt, but what some inquisitive traveller might still meet with manifest traces of it in many parts of the Pyrenaeans and other mountainous regions of Spain, where the Moors and other invaders have never penetrated.

I have the honour to be, &c.

*　　*　　*　　*　　*

## # NO. I. OATH OF LEWIS THE GERMANIC. #

| 1. Latin from which the Romances are derived. | 2. Gallic Romance in which the oath was taken. | 3. French of the twelfth century. | 4. Romansh of Engadine, called Ladin. | 5. Romansh of both dialects. |
|---|---|---|---|---|
| 1. Pro Dei amore, et pro Christiano populo, et nostro | 2. *Pro Deu amur, et pro Christian poblo, et nostro* | 3. Por Deu amor, et por Christian people, et nostre | 4. *Per amur da Dieu, et per il Christian poevel, et noss* | 5. Pro l'amur da Deus, et pro il Christian pobel, et nost |
| 1. communi salvamento, de ista die in abante, in quan- | 2. *commun salvament, d'ist di en avant, in quant* | 3. commun salvament, de ste di en avant, en quant | 4. *commun salvament, da quist di in avant, in quant* | 5. commun salvament, d'ist di en avant, in quant |
| 1.tum Deus sapere et posse mihi donat, sic salvabo ego | 2. *Deus savir et podir me dunat, si salvarai io* | 3. Deu saveir et poïr me donne, si salvarai je | 4. *Dieu savair et podair m'duna, shi salvaro ei* | 5. Deus savir et podir m'dunat, shi salvaro io |
| 1. eccistum meum fratrem Karlum, et in adjutum ero | 2. *cist meon fradre Karlo, et in adjudab er* | 3. cist mon frere Karle, et en adjude serai | 4. *quist mieu fræer Carlo, et in adgiud li saro* | 5. quist meu frad'r Carl, et in adjudh saro |
| 1. in quaque una causa, sic quomodo homo per directum | 2. *in cadhuna cosa, si cum on per dreit* | 3. en cascune cose, si cum on per dreict | 4. *in chiaduna chiossa, shi seho l'hom per drett* | 5. in caduna cosa, si com om per drett |
| 1. suum fratrem salvare debet, in hoc quod ille mihi | 2. *son fardre salvar dist, in o quid il me* | 3. son frere salver dist, en o qui il me | 4. *sieu fræer salvar d'uess, in que chél a mi* | 5. seu frad'r salvar dess, in que chél me |

| | | | | |
|---|---|---|---|---|
| 1. alterum sic faceret; et ab Lothario nullum placitum | 2. *altresi fazet; et ab Laudher nul plaid* | 3. altresi fascet; et a Lothaire nul plaid | 4. *altresi fadschess; et da Lothar mai non paendrò io un* | 5. altresi fazess; et da Lothar nul plaid mai |
| 1. nunquam prehendam quod meo volle eccisti meo fratri | 2. *nunquam prindrai qui meon vol cist meon fradre* | 3. nonques prendrai qui par mon voil a cist mon frere | 4. *plæd che con mieu volair a quist mieu frær* | 5. non prendro che con meu voler a quist meu frad'r |
| 1. Karlo in damno sit. | 2. *Karle in domno sit.* | 3. Karle en dam seit. | 4. *Carlo sai in damn.* | 5. Carl in damn sia. |

*    *    *    *    *

# # NO. II. THE FIRST PARAGRAPH OF THE LAWS OF WILLIAM THE CONQUEROR. #

| 1. The Latin translation. | 2. The French original. | 3. A translation into the Romansh of both dialects. |
|---|---|---|
| 1. Hae sunt Leges et Consuetudines quas Willelmus Rex | 2. *Ce sont les Leis et les Custumes que li Reis William grantut* | 3. Que sun las Leias e'ls Custums que il Rei Willelm ga- |
| 1. concessit toto populo Angliæ post subactam terram | 2. *a tut le peuple de Engleterre aprés le conquest de la terre* | 3. rantit a tut il poevel d'Engelterra dapo il conquist della |
| 1. Eædem sut quas Edwardus Rex Cognatus ejus obser- | 2. *Ice les meismes que la Reis Edward sun Cosin tint* | 3. terra. E sun las medemas que il Rei Edward su cusrin |
| 1. vavit ante eum. Scilicet: Pax Sanctæ Ecclesiæ, | 2. *devant lui. Co est a saveir: Pais a Sainte Eglise,* | 3. tenet avant el. Co es da savir: Pæsh alla Sainta Ba- |
| 1. cujuscunque forisfacturae quis reus sit hoc tempore, et | 2. *de quel forfait que home out fait en cel tens, et* | 3. selg.[*] da quel sfarfatt que om a fatt en que tem, et |
| 1. venire potest ad sanctum: Ecclesiam, pacem habeat vitae | 2. *il pout venir a sainte Eglise, out pais de vie* | 3. il pout venir alla Sainta Baselga, haun pæsh da vitta |
| 1. et membri. Et si quis injecerit manum in eum qui 2. *et de membre. E se alquons meist main en celui qui* | 3. et da members. E si alcun metta man a quel que la | |

1. matrem Ecclesiam quaesierit, sive sit Abbatia sive

2. *la mere Eglise requireit, se ceo fust u Abbeie u*

3. mamma Baselga requira, qu'ella fuss Abbatia u

1. Ecclesia religionis, reddat eum quem abstulerit et

2. *Eglise de religion, rendist ce que il javereit pris*

3. Baselga da religiun, renda que qu'el savares prais, et

1. centum solides nomine forisfacturae, et matri Ecclesiae

2. *e cent sols de forfait, e de Mer Eglise de*

3. cent solds da sfarfatt, et alla mamma Baselga da

1. parochiali 20 solidos, et capellae 10 solidos: Et qui fregerit

2. *paroisse 20 solds, e de Chapelle 10 solds; E que enfraiant*

3. parochia 20 solds, e da capella 10 solds: E que in frignand

1. pacem Regis in Merchenelega 100 solidis emendet;

2. *la pais le Rei en Merchenelae 100 solds les amendes;*

3. la pæsh del Rei in Merchenelae 100 solds d'amenda;

1. similiter de compensatione homicidii et de insidiis

2. *altresi de Heinfare e de aweit*

3. altresi della compensatiun del omicidi et insidias

1. præcogitatis.

2. *purpensed.*

3. perpensadas.

*    *    *    *    *

# ENDNOTES

[*]   The word Ecclesia being more modern in the Latin tongue than *Basilica*, the Romansh word Baselga derived from the latter is an additional proof of the antiquity of this language.

Lector House believes that a society develops through a two-fold approach of continuous learning and adaptation, which is derived from the study of classic literary works spread across the historic timeline of literature records. Therefore, we aim at reviving, repairing and redeveloping all those inaccessible or damaged but historically as well as culturally important literature across subjects so that the future generations may have an opportunity to study and learn from past works to embark upon a journey of creating a better future.

This book is a result of an effort made by Lector House towards making a contribution to the preservation and repair of original ancient works which might hold historical significance to the approach of continuous learning across subjects.

**HAPPY READING & LEARNING!**

**LECTOR HOUSE LLP**
**E-MAIL: lectorpublishing@gmail.com**